Developing and Maintaining a Sexual Harassment-Free Workplace

A Guide for Managers
Second Edition

David J. Bassham

Developing and Maintaining a Sexual Harassment-Free Workplace
A Guide for Managers
2nd Edition

David Bassham

ISBN 1-929728-04-2

*For information on ordering additional copies
of this book or other books by this authors, please
visit www.bassham-rayl.com.*

About the Author

David J. Bassham is a training, education and counseling professional with broad experience in training adults in a variety of professional and organizational development areas surrounding interpersonal relationship skills as well as other human resource related areas. As the principal in Bassham & Associates, he has provided speaking, training and consulting on sexual harassment and other human resource related topics since 1998.

He is a former Associate Professor at DeVry University and has extensive experience in teaching a diverse adult population on various subjects, including psychology, sociology, critical thinking, human relations, leadership and motivation. David received his M.S. in Psychology at the University of North Texas and his B.S. in Sociology from the University of the State of New York. As a former Licensed Psychological Associate in the State of Texas, he has extensive clinical experience including conducting psychological evaluations, diagnostic clinical interviewing and structured behavioral observation.

In addition, Bassham & Associates has provided training for diverse clients such as Southwest Airlines, PepsiCo, Astra Zeneca Pharmaceuticals, U.S. Department of Agriculture, Clark Cincinnati Steel, U.S. Department of Education, Social Security Administration, U.S. Forest Service, El Centro College, U.S. Pretrial Services, Mary Kay and other government, educational and corporate clients.

David has been a volunteer presenter for the Center for Nonprofit Management in Dallas and served as a member of the curriculum development team and presenter for the Dallas Non-profit Entrepreneur Academy. He is Past-President of the Board of Trustees of the Citizens Development Center, a non-profit agency that provides vocational and rehabilitation services to handicapped adults.

Disclaimer

The purpose of this booklet is to educate and provide a framework for providing a better workplace. It should in no way be construed as a substitute for competent legal counsel. The authors and publisher shall have neither liability nor responsibility to any person or entity with respect to any loss or damage caused, or alleged to be caused, directly or indirectly by the information contained in this book.

If you do not wish to be bound by the above, you may return this book to the publisher for a full refund.

Acknowledgements

A lot of the credit for this book goes to my wife Karen for her insights, suggestions and tireless proofreading efforts. Without which, no one would have understood the message I was trying to convey. A special thanks also goes to my dear friend Dr. Anne Gervasi for reviewing the final work and providing a much needed additional pair of eyes to the process.

Table of Contents

> *"Nobody will ever win the Battle of the Sexes. There is just too much fraternizing with the enemy."*

Henry Kissinger, Diplomat

Introduction

When I wrote the original version of this book in 2000, my objective was to provide not only the legal definitions and implications of sexual harassment, but also an easy-to-follow guide for what organizations could do to prevent sexual harassment and limit their liability should they face litigation if it did occur. In the aftermath of the landmark 1998 U.S. Supreme Court rulings concerning employer liability in sexual harassment cases, I saw a business environment ill-equipped to deal with sexual harassment complaints, let alone do the things necessary to prevent harassment in the first place.

I also saw a world in which high-profile cases involving sexual harassment were commonplace. For example, in 1991, during his confirmation hearings, U.S. Supreme Court Justice Clarence Thomas, the former head of the Equal Employment Opportunity Commission (the agency responsible for enforcing the Civil Rights Act of 1964, including Title VII) was accused of sexually harassing his assistant, Anita Hill, while head of that agency. In 1994, Paula Jones sued President Bill Clinton for sexual harassment while he was Governor of the State of Arkansas. And the list goes on.

It was becoming increasingly clear that the work-a-day world we knew was changing forever. Businesses large and small were developing sexual harassment policies and training their employees. Zero tolerance was becoming the current corporate catch phrase. The Courts and the EEOC were handing down large judgments against those organizations that were slow to respond to the changes in the corporate climate of this country. From all appearances, the end of sexual harassment was in sight.

Yet here we are, eight years later, and I am busier than ever before. I am still working with organizations that have woefully inadequate sexual harassment policies, poor mechanisms in place to disseminate those policies, and haphazard training programs to educate their employees and managers. I generally get called in after they have had a sexual harassment complaint. So, yes, here we are eight years later and an updated version of this book is necessary.

Whether an organization faces sexual harassment litigation or not, it is still important to take the steps necessary to prevent the harassment because it has been found to cause, not only public embarrassment, but also monetary losses from health claims, and loss of employee productivity. Add in the considerable financial loss resulting from lawsuits, even if the organization is found to be not liable, and the question is not *should* employers take reasonable steps to prevent or correct promptly any sexually harassing behavior, but more *how* do they take those reasonable steps.

The 1998 U.S. Supreme Court cases, (see Appendix A) have held employer's responsible for the actions of not only their managers but for the actions of their employees and even individuals not in their employ who engage in sexually harassing behavior. For instance, if an employee other than a supervisor engages in hostile environment sexual harassment, the company is liable if they knew about it (or should have known about it) and failed to take appropriate action. If the employee is a supervisor, the company is liable whether they knew or not. Secondly, claimants are no longer required to prove that the employer was negligent in preventing sexual harassment. This means that the employer can no longer use ignorance of the events as a defense against liability.

Finally, and perhaps most importantly, the Court shifted emphasis from whether a supervisor's action was conditioned on a job benefit to whether the harassment resulted in a tangible employment action, such as demotion or discharge. When the supervisor's behavior results in such actions, there is no defense against employer liability. If, on the other hand, there is no resulting impact on the claimant's employment status, then the employer has an affirmative defense available. The two necessary elements to this affirmative defense are reasonable care on the part of the employer *to prevent or correct promptly any sexually harassing behavior*, and an *unreasonable failure* on the part of the claimant to utilize the mechanisms provided by the employer to protect employees against harm.

The two most recent U.S. Supreme Court rulings clarified the application of the affirmative defense in cases involving *constructive discharge**, and broadened the scope of retaliation to include acts outside tangible employment action that would discourage a reasonable employee from filing a complaint of sexual harassment or from participating in the investigation of such complaint (see Appendix A.)

In the last ten years of providing consulting and training to companies and organizations of various types and sizes, I have learned a lot about how sexual harassment occurs and the kind of mistakes companies make in handling complaints. The first edition of this book covered all of the bases on the topic but, hopefully, this revision will clear up some of the gray areas and allow me to share some of the things I have learned about how to stay out of court.

Appendix A contains information concerning the U.S. Supreme Court rulings that address sexual harassment and, in particular, employer liability. Appendix B contains a sample sexual harassment policy that could serve as a guide for developing a policy.

The information contained in these chapters is intended to provide guidelines for developing policies and procedures that will help to reduce the likelihood of company liability should litigation occur and **should in no way be construed to be a substitute for competent legal counsel.**

---

*Constructive Discharge: "A termination of employment brought about by making the employee's working conditions so intolerable that the employee feels compelled to leave." —*Black's Law Dictionary*,

> *"You're only as good as your information."*

Bob Seger, American singer/songwriter

Chapter 1
Legal definitions, descriptions and other
necessary evils

What is sexual harassment?

Unless one has been living in a cave these last few decades, he or she is quite aware of the term "sexual harassment." The phrase has gained tremendous visibility with high-profile cases in government, schools, churches and corporations. Many people reading the newspapers or listening to television newscasts will see at least one reported story two or three times a month, if not more. They may shake their heads in disgust when they see it, sometimes at the accused, sometimes even at the victim, and sometimes at the circumstances that allowed it to happen in the first place.

With all of the public attention, it is not surprising that most people seem to have a fairly good understanding of what actually constitutes sexual harassment and how prevalent it is. It is common to see in sexual harassment training that all but the youngest employees have attended at least one prior training session and are very familiar with the material.

Still, when talking to individuals who have been accused of sexual harassment, many of them are surprised that what they have done fits within the definition of sexual harassment. Frequently, what they have done fits in the "gray areas" where perception rules and the surprise is genuine. At other times, their surprise can legitimately be attributed to denial.

What Constitutes Sexual Harassment?

In 1980, the EEOC released guidelines that included sexual harassment as a civil rights violation under Title VII of the Civil Rights Act of 1964. These guidelines describe sexual harassment as a form of sex discrimination and define two types of sexual harassment: *"quid pro quo"* and *"hostile environment."*

Quid pro quo

"Quid pro quo" was initially probably the more well-known of the two definitions of the types of harassment. The term, which comes from the Latin and means roughly "this for that," involves unwelcome sexual advances, requests for sexual favors, and other verbal or physical conduct of a sexual nature "when:

- such conduct is made either explicitly or implicitly a term or condition of an individual's employment, or
- submission to or rejection of such conduct by an individual is used as the basis for employment decisions affecting such individual."

An example of this would be if a manager, or someone with power, tells job candidates or employees that if they do some sexual favor (such as go away with him or her for the weekend, spend the night, kiss, touch, talk "dirty," and so forth) then the manager will hire the person or make the person's job better. The Court has ruled that this type of harassment must contain some form of tangible employment action.

Hostile Environment

While "hostile environment" sexual harassment has a legal definition from the EEOC, much more is left open to interpretation. This type of sexual harassment involves "unwelcome sexual advances, requests for sexual favors, and other verbal or physical conduct of a sexual nature when such conduct has the purpose or effect of unreasonably interfering with an individual's work performance or creating an intimidating, hostile, or offensive working environment."

The confusion around hostile environment sexual harassment is that it doesn't necessarily have to be about sex. While dirty jokes, sexual innuendo, and so on, can clearly constitute hostile environment sexual harassment, harassment of an individual based on their gender (including sexual orientation) could also be considered sexual harassment if it is severe enough to interfere with that individual's working environment or performance.

A manager who treats different employees in different ways may just be a bad manager and, unfortunately, that is not against the law. If that manager groups people by their gender (or race, or age, or nationality), that is against the law and can constitute hostile environment harassment, sexual or otherwise.

The "meat" of an investigation into a hostile environment complaint is in whether the conduct "unreasonably interfered with an individual's work performance" or created "an intimidating, hostile, or offensive working environment." The EEOC looks at the following factors to determine whether an environment is hostile:

- Whether the conduct was verbal or physical or both;
- How frequently it was repeated;
- Whether the conduct was hostile or patently offensive;
- Whether the alleged harasser was a co-worker or supervisor;
- Whether others joined in perpetrating the harassment; and
- Whether the harassment was directed at more than one individual.

The assessment is made based upon the totality of the circumstances with all factors being considered. For instance, when considered individually, a series of harassing behaviors might not be considered severe enough to constitute a hostile environment, but taken as a whole, they might well be. Simply telling someone they look nice today would not be considered harassment, whereas telling them they look nice ten times in one day could be.

Hostile environment cases have involved such things as accusations of sexual jokes and innuendo, sexually explicit pictures posted in an office, tone of voice and suggestive looks, etc. If the person making the accusation feels that, through this behavior, he or she has been put into a hostile environment that undermines the ability to do the job, he or she can make a complaint.

"Reasonable Woman" Standard
The courts have introduced what is called the "Reasonable Woman" standard, which is based on the assumption that what a man considers harassment and what a woman considers harassment are "widely divergent" according to research findings. Sexual harassment of women,

according to the courts is, therefore, "conduct which a 'reasonable woman' would consider sufficiently severe or pervasive to alter the conditions of employment and cause an abusive working environment."

The next logical question is, of course, who defines a "reasonable woman." Some researchers also question just how "widely divergent" perspectives actually are between men and women, but most will admit that differences in perspectives do exist. Courts have ruled that "in evaluating the severity and pervasiveness of sexual harassment, they must focus on the perspective of the victim (frequently a woman)."

Who can be a victim of sexual harassment?
The victim may be a woman or a man and does not have to be of the opposite sex from the offender. While the majority of sexual harassment cases involve male-to-female sexual harassment, any gender combinations are possible and, indeed, occur (see *Oncale v. Sundowner* in Appendix A). In addition, the victim does not have to be the person actually harassed but could be anyone *affected* by the offensive conduct.

Who can be a sexual harasser?
The harasser may be a woman or a man. And, contrary to what many people think, in addition to the victim's supervisor, the harasser could be an agent of the employer, a supervisor in another area, a co-worker, or an individual not employed by the company. In the case of the latter, the fact the harasser doesn't work for the company doesn't relieve the company of the responsibility to protect its employees from harassment. Some examples are customers, vendors, and delivery people. Companies tend to become conflicted when the harasser is their best customer. Fearing the loss of revenue, they frequently turn a blind eye to the complaint which only leaves them vulnerable to a law suit that will likely cost many times the revenue they might have lost.

Chapter 2
Prevalence and costs of sexual harassment

Organizations must realize that while lawsuits and image damage may be the most obvious and potentially the most costly outcomes, they are not the only byproduct of sexual harassment. Health claims, low morale, reduced productivity, tardiness, absenteeism, as well as negative employee retention can lead to even higher costs to the employer as a result of sexual harassment. The only way to avoid these costs is to ensure that sexual harassment is effectively addressed with policies, procedures, sexual harassment awareness education for all employees and specialized training for managers in handling sexual harassment complaints.

Research has shown that between 40 and 60 percent of women have experienced some form of harassing behavior. While not all these experiences meet legal criteria for sexual harassment, they can lead to depression, anxiety and stress-related physical problems, particularly when the harassment is frequent and intense. In addition, job satisfaction may be negatively affected by harassment. Furthermore, about ten percent of women who are sexually harassed leave their jobs. While this may have changed to some extent over the last ten years, there are still enough examples available to support those findings.

Also, while nearly half of North American women experience harassment within a two-year time period, the rates go up in the "male culture" work environments, such as manufacturing. Research in the late 1990s shows that women working in these traditional male environments are particularly vulnerable to hostile work environment sexual harassment as well as physical abuse.

Avoidance is the most common effect of harassment. Many individuals report that unwanted sexual attention interferes with their work performance because they avoid work or other situations where they encounter the harasser. This means a victim may miss days of work, not go to important meetings, miss deadlines, and lose productivity because of the sexual harassment they are facing. This can cause the victim considerable stress and disruption when he or she alters activities to avoid the harasser.

As the EEOC and State Fair Employment Practices Agencies (FEPA's) have recently reported, claims of sexual harassment have decreased by around 20 percent compared to 1998 levels though the number of cases settled has remained relatively constant in that time. In that same timeframe, the monetary benefits paid to complainants has tended to remain relatively stable at approximately $50 million a year. That amount does not include legal fees and the other tangible as well as intangible costs associated with a sexual harassment case.

While these claims are pending, they can weaken company management and work relationships. The process of dealing with sexual harassment claims is very disruptive, not only for the principals involved, but for all of the other employees caught up in making statements, testifying, and having to deal with the behaviors of those involved.

Negative effects on the workplace sometimes far outlast the dispute itself, and the cost of litigation may be modest compared to the business costs of a real harassment problem. Not only can employee morale and productivity be compromised, but also managers will be distracted from revenue-producing functions, and in severe situations, company performance and profitability may decline. Supreme Court rulings have made it clear that organizations can be held liable for the workplace behavior of employees and for not maintaining workplace standards and practices that discourage sexual harassment.

The obvious conclusion is that organizations must have effective policies concerning sexual harassment, comprehensive training programs for conveying that policy to all employees, mechanisms in place for reporting complaints, and an established procedure for investigating and resolving complaints promptly. While establishing and maintaining these policies and procedures may not completely shield the organization from litigation, they will provide the only protection available in such cases (see *Ellerth v. Burlington Industries* and *Faragher v. Boca Raton* in Appendix A)

The prevalence of sexual harassment in a work organization is influenced by several factors:

- **Employee's perceptions** of how harassment is tolerated in the work environment affect the likelihood that employees will come forward with reports of sexually harassing behaviors. If an employee feels they will be taken seriously if they make a complaint, they will be much more likely to come forward. Obviously, there are a number of management issues involved in creating that perception but taking every complaint seriously is a good place to start.
- **The perceptions of the consequences** of those behaviors affect the likelihood of individuals engaging in sexually harassing behaviors. There are probably few things management can do to stop a "sexual predator" type harasser from harassing someone, but clearly spelled out consequences for inappropriate workplace behavior, including termination, come as close as anything. *Besides, the vast majority of employees are not sexual predators.*
- **The level of commitment among the organization's managers** to effectively handle harassment problems contributes to how policies and procedures are implemented to combat the problem. Managers who merely pay lip service to sexual harassment policies send the message to harassers as well as victims that complaints of sexual harassment will not be taken seriously.
- **Education** ensures that managers and employees alike understand the problem and see that their organization's management is trying to control harassing behavior. Regular (at least yearly) sexual awareness training for managers and employees makes a clear statement as to the organization's level of commitment to preventing sexual harassment as well as reducing the likelihood that harassment will occur and increasing the probability that the victim will come forward with a complaint if it does. In addition, regular training for managers on how to handle complaints goes a long way toward ensuring that every complaint is taken seriously and handled appropriately, which reduces the possibility of litigation.

> *"What lies in our power to do,*
> *it lies in our power not to do."*

Aristotle, philosopher

Chapter 3
The written policy: the first step in preventing litigation

The landmark U.S. Supreme Court rulings in 1998 provided employers an affirmative defense if they show that they "exercised reasonable care to prevent and correct promptly any sexually harassing behavior." However, the definition and criteria for *reasonable care* are still subject to interpretation by the courts.

Legal experts seem, generally, to be in agreement that as a minimum companies need to maintain a strong, effective sexual harassment policy, provide periodic awareness training, position mechanisms to provide recourse for victims, and establish a procedure for handling and investigating complaints.

While all four of these are important in their own right, the written policy supplies the foundation for the other three. It should provide guidelines for what the organization considers to be acceptable or unacceptable conduct, procedures for employees to report instances of harassment, and steps for management to follow in dealing with complaints.

Describe harassing behaviors
To be effective, a written sexual harassment policy must contain explicit language that indicates the organization will not tolerate sexual harassment. It is important that the policy describes in detail the different types of sexual harassment and the behavior that constitutes each type of sexual harassment. While it may seem obvious to human resources professionals what types of behaviors constitute sexual harassment, not everyone has this same level of awareness. The sad truth is that, in the absence of some previous sexual harassment awareness

training, most employees would be hard pressed to define either *quid pro quo* or *hostile environment* sexual harassment, let alone identify examples of either. Even those employees who have had previous awareness training don't do particularly well at identifying most of the more subtle examples of sexual harassment.

Providing examples of each type of sexual harassment is helpful. While examples of male-to-female sexual harassment are the most likely form to be encountered in the workplace, examples of harassment with female-to-male, same-sex and individuals who are not in the employ of the company should also be included.

Outline the reporting procedure
The policy should outline a clear, understandable procedure that will allow and encourage employees to report harassing behavior regardless of whether that specific behavior is clearly described in the policy or not. This procedure should allow for some latitude as to which members of management the employee must report the objectionable behavior to should that situation arise. The fewer the number of choices employees have, the less likely they are to report an incident.

Some employees are more comfortable talking about such issues with males than females and vice versa. Others would be more comfortable reporting this type of incident to a stranger than to their manager. In the worst case scenario, if the manager to whom the complaint should be reported is the one engaging in the sexually harassing behavior, it is unlikely that management would learn of the harassment until the lawsuit or EEOC complaint was filed.

There should be explicit language indicating that all reports will be kept confidential. In addition, it should be made clear that the company will not allow retaliation toward anyone who files a sexual harassment complaint or participates in the investigation and that retaliation is also subject to disciplinary action up to and including termination.

Clearly state the disciplinary policy
A clear statement of the company's disciplinary policy with regard

to sexual harassment should be included in the written policy. It must be clearly spelled out that engaging in sexually harassing behavior carries with it serious consequences. Research has clearly shown that individuals who are prone to engage in such behaviors will continue to do so in spite of their awareness of the company's sexual harassment policy if they perceive that policy to be ineffective or lacking in significant consequences. While all acts of sexual harassment are not of similar severity, the policy must allow for different alternatives in the types of discipline available to management to ensure that the punishment is commensurate with the offense. At the very minimum, it should be clearly stated that engaging in sexually harassing behavior may be grounds for discharge with the severity and frequency of the offense(s) increasing that likelihood.

Provide procedure for complaint handling
The policy should outline a procedure for management to follow in handling complaints and, subsequently, investigating each complaint. The way the company handles a complaint initially has considerable bearing upon whether the company is seen as taking *reasonable care* to promptly correct inappropriate conduct.

Beyond that, the speed and manner in which complaints are investigated are equally important. How the investigator is chosen, whether the investigator is a member of management or an independent third party, and the responsibilities and authority of the investigator in conducting the investigation should all be clearly defined.

It is important to have a well thought out procedure for initial complaint handling and investigation *before* a complaint is registered. A plan of action created in the midst of the emotional turmoil that may surround a complaint leaves the company vulnerable to a variety of mistakes that can significantly increase the likelihood of litigation and subsequent company liability.

While some organizations may prefer to include this procedure separately in their policies and procedures, companies should consider including it within the sexual harassment policy to let employees know what to expect from the organization should they file a complaint.

Describe management's role in complaint handling and investigation

Include well-defined authority and responsibilities for members of management with regard to the initial handling of complaints, as well as their participation in the resulting investigations, in the policy. Members of management should have a good understanding of their responsibilities in such cases and the severity of the consequences for the company should they fail to follow the designated procedures. This section should also include details of disciplinary action that may result from their failure to follow those procedures. While this section does not necessarily have to be in the sexual harassment policy, it should exist somewhere in the organization's policies and procedures.

Explain how the policy will be communicated

Finally, the company's sexual harassment policy should clearly describe how the information contained within the policy will be disseminated to management and the employees. Provisions for posting and distributing copies of the policy to all employees should be delineated in detail along with methods for ensuring all employees have been provided with the policy.

In addition, detailed plans for periodic sexual awareness training for all employees as well as management training explaining the procedures for initial complaint handling and investigations should be included.

As is the case with any company policy, the perceived effectiveness of the policy is not determined by the words on the paper. Management's actions in implementing and enforcing the policy will ultimately determine the perceived effectiveness of the policy in the eyes of the employees and possibly in the eyes of the courts. Considering the potentially high cost involved in the failure to apply an effective sexual harassment policy, it becomes clear that companies can no longer afford to ignore the issue.

Appendix B contains a sample Sexual Harassment Policy.

"Knowledge itself is power."

Sir Francis Bacon, English philosopher, essayist, statesman

Chapter 4
Now that you have a policy, how do you let everyone know about it?

While it is clear that a comprehensive and well-written sexual harassment policy is essential for an employer to have a good defense against litigation, it won't be effective if employees are not aware of it. The policy must be disseminated to all employees, regardless of their relative position within the company, and records to this effect must be kept. These records should include a signed statement indicating that they have received and read the policy (see *Faragher v. Boca Raton* in Appendix A). If it isn't written down, it didn't happen!

However, simply handing employees a copy of the company's sexual harassment policy and getting a signature does not ensure they will read it, let alone understand it. Sexual harassment awareness training should be provided to all employees and, once again, records to that effect should be kept. This will provide another piece of tangible evidence to support an employer's claim that they have made a reasonable effort to *prevent or promptly* correct sexual harassment should they be faced with litigation.

Unfortunately, a single lecture or workshop is unlikely to be viewed by the courts as a good faith effort on the part of the employer. This becomes especially true as the length of time since the lecture or workshop increases. Most legal experts recommend that each employee should attend one or two mandatory sexual harassment awareness training sessions per year. While this certainly entails what could be a sizable investment, depending upon the number of employees, the costs are negligible when compared to the potential cost of sexual harassment litigation even if the company is not held liable.

Why is training important?

Other than proving to the courts that your company has made a reasonable effort to prevent sexual harassment, what else can good sexual harassment training provide?

- It will provide employees and supervisors alike with clear descriptions of the types of behaviors that are appropriate and inappropriate. In the absence of this type of training, most people have only a vague idea of the types of behaviors that constitute sexual harassment.
- It can ensure the effective communication of the sexual harassment policy to all employees and emphasize the employer's position on preventing sexual harassment.
- It can provide employees with a clear understanding of the established complaint procedure and what they can expect from the company should they file a complaint.
- It can educate members of management in the appropriate steps to take when confronted with a sexual harassment complaint. (Additional training should be provided for managers to ensure they understand how to handle complaints and the importance of doing so.)

Taken together, training in these areas can go a long way toward preventing or eliminating sexual harassment in the workplace. Should sexually harassing behavior occur in spite of the training, it is still more likely that management will react appropriately which, in turn, should reduce the likelihood of litigation.

———————————

AUTHOR'S NOTE

While there has been a growing trend over the last ten years toward video, computer-based and Internet-based training for sexual harassment (and virtually every other training topic), my experience has been that this is the least effective approach to educating employees and managers about sexual harassment. While many of these programs, especially the more recent ones, are very well done, their effectiveness is directly proportional to the level of motivation of the viewer.

Typically what I have found is once people find themselves in trouble they are much more interested in the topic. I recently did some remedial training with an individual that had been accused of hostile work environment sexual harassment. His company uses a video training program and part of his remedial training was to view this video (again) and go through one-on-one sexual harassment counseling. When I asked what he got out of the video he told me that he "got a lot more out of it this time because I paid attention this time."

Who should conduct this training?

Many larger companies use their in-house training or human resources staff to provide this training. Some smaller companies have managers conduct this training. Many times both large and small companies rely on outside training professionals to handle this sensitive training. This sometimes helps to provide that important third-party unbiased tone. However, if an outside party provides the training, the company should show its commitment to the training by having a senior executive come in at the beginning to introduce the session and emphasize how important it is.

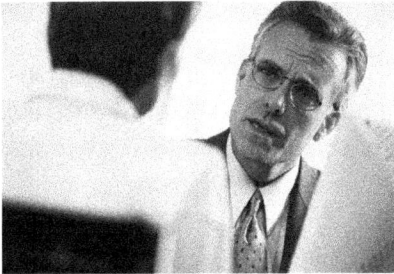

What are the training objectives?

When developing a sexual harassment training program, the following general objectives should be considered. The training should provide:

- A clear understanding of the company's written sexual harassment policy.
- Clear definitions of the different forms of sexual harassment with several examples to illustrate each.
- A working knowledge of the mechanisms provided in the written policy for reporting incidents of sexual harassment (including to whom incidents should be reported) as well as the mechanisms provided to protect employees who make such complaints.

- Specific elaboration on the company's discipline policy as it applies to sexual harassment.
- Written evaluations of each individual employee's understanding of the company's written sexual harassment policy, what constitutes inappropriate conduct, the disciplinary consequences for such behavior, and the mechanisms in place to report such behaviors. This can generally take the form of a short test.
- Detailed instructions for managers and supervisory personnel for handling sexual harassment complaints and the subsequent investigations.

Managers need additional training

With the exception of the final one, the objectives listed above could provide the practical basis for a training program for all employees including management and supervisory personnel. However, it is clear that management and supervisory personnel require additional training that does not necessarily apply to employees in general.

These individuals are directly responsible for implementing and enforcing the employer's policy as well as being the first line of defense against sexual harassment litigation. Consequently, additional training should be provided to individuals who manage/supervise employees to ensure that they:
- Have a clear understanding of what constitutes inappropriate behavior, how to spot those behaviors and how to stop them.
- Refrain from engaging in inappropriate behavior at all times and understand the disciplinary consequences for failing to do so.
- Clearly understand the legal implications of sexual harassment for the company.
- Respond immediately to every employee complaint of sexual harassment.
- Understand the importance of appropriately handling an initial employee complaint.
- Know the requirements for reporting employee complaints or incidents of inappropriate behavior.
- Take every step necessary to safeguard the confidentiality of each report and to protect the employee making the report from possible retaliation.

Research shows training works

Research in this area suggests that many of the minor forms of sexually harassing behavior can be prevented or eliminated simply by making employees aware that these behaviors constitute sexual harassment. The research also suggests that the likelihood of the more serious forms of sexual harassment can be reduced through training and the presence of proactive mechanisms for dealing with these behaviors.

Therefore, it should be clear that a well-developed, properly implemented and documented sexual harassment awareness training program, combined with an effective sexual harassment policy with mechanisms to protect employees, will contribute significantly to maintaining a sexual-harassment-free workplace. At the very least, they will provide the employer with tangible evidence that they have made a reasonable effort to prevent or promptly remedy any incidents of sexual harassment.

In response to the U.S. Supreme Court rulings in 1998 (See Ellerth and Faragher in Appendix A), which clarified the liability of employers in sexual harassment cases, most responsible companies have instituted some form of regular sexual harassment training program for their employees and managers. In 2004, California passed *Assembly Bill 1825*, which requires companies with more than 50 employees conduct at least two hours of sexual harassment training for each of its supervisory employees every two years. This law also sets a specific quality standard for the training (requirements listed in *California Government Code 12950.1)*. Connecticut and Maine have similar laws requiring sexual harassment training, but they do not have specific requirements for how the training should be delivered.

"In a world of growing complexity, leaders are increasingly dependent on their subordinates for good information, whether the leaders want to hear it or not. Followers who tell the truth and leaders who listen to it are an unbeatable combination."

Warren G. Bennis, American writer, educator, sociologist

Chapter 5
Handling the initial complaint: the first step in resolving the problem or the pathway to litigation?

Once you have an effective sexual harassment policy and a well-developed training plan, you are almost there. However, neither are more than mere "lip-service" if complaints are not handled in a fair and timely manner.

When you consider that reporting an incident of sexual harassment to a manager or supervisor is a very difficult and uncomfortable thing for an employee to do in the first place, the importance of handling that complaint promptly and in a professional manner increases dramatically. Most employees who report instances of sexual harassment do so, generally, only after the harassment has continued for some period of time and has caused a significant level of distress. Mishandled complaints put the employee in a precarious position at best, which may prompt them to seek relief in the form of a lawsuit or EEOC/FEPA complaint. Needless to say, neither of these is in the employer's best interest.

The way the complaint is handled initially is critical to how the employee (and possibly the court) perceives the employer's interest in preventing and/or eliminating sexually harassing behavior. What follows are several simple guidelines for managers faced with an employee with a sexual harassment complaint.

Take every complaint seriously.
While every situation is different, an effective sexual harassment policy dictates that **each complaint** be thoroughly investigated. The shortest path to litigation is to dismiss the complaint without gathering

and considering all of the facts regardless of the situation or individuals involved. Even if the employee asks that no formal action be taken, management has, at that point, been made aware of the situation and can be vulnerable to litigation if they do not take remedial action.

However, organizations differ. If the company procedure spells out who should take the initial complaint, when an employee with a complaint approaches any manager or supervisor that manager or supervisor becomes *personally responsible* for ensuring that the employee connects with the person designated to take the complaint. That means walk the individual down to HR or to the appropriate person's office.

Maintain a professional and impartial attitude.
To the greatest extent possible, managers should not become personally involved in the situation. Taking sides without carefully evaluating the facts can be dangerous. Taking the side of the perpetrator without a thorough investigation is not the only danger in this situation. Taking the side of the "victim" without a thorough investigation can possibly lead to defamation litigation against the company and the employee who reported it.

Every effort should be made to prevent preconceived ideas and attitudes about the individuals involved and the work environment from biasing the information gathered in this initial session. The perceived credibility of the participants in this situation should not influence whether or not the complaint is handled in accordance with the company's sexual harassment policy. Every complaint is serious and should be investigated. A manager that has a personal involvement with any of the parties involved (whether that involvement is public knowledge or not) may not appear to be impartial should that involvement become known. In such cases, a different individual should take the complaint.

Maintain confidentiality throughout the proceedings.
Considerable damage can be done to the reputations of the individuals involved if information concerning the complaint is given an open forum. Management has a responsibility to protect the individuals involved in the complaint. Additionally, releasing this type of information can have a disruptive effect on the productivity of the organization in general as well as an impact on perspective witnesses.

Assure prompt remedial action and protection from retaliation.
Assure the employee reporting the incident that the company will take prompt action to correct the problem if misconduct is found, and he or she will be protected from any form of retaliation as a result of making the complaint. Determine whether action needs to be taken to protect the employee from retaliation and take that action immediately, if necessary. The fear of worsening the situation or job loss is likely to be significant in the mind of the employee reporting the harassment. Successfully allaying those fears goes a long way toward building the perception that the company is interested in preventing and/or eliminating sexually harassing behavior, which in turn, may significantly reduce the likelihood of later litigation.

Gather as much pertinent information as possible.
Make an attempt to answer all of the journalistic questions of who, what, where, when, why, and how. Who was involved and who saw it? What exactly was said or done? Where did it happen? When did it occur? Why was it considered to be harassing? How did they respond? In addition, is there any hard evidence such as memos, notes, e-mail, etc.? Get as much specific information and get it in writing if at all possible.

Ensure the complaint is promptly passed on to the designated individual.
All of the information gathered in the initial phase of the reporting procedure should be forwarded immediately to the person responsible for investigating sexual harassment complaints as designated in the company's sexual harassment policy.

Most importantly, effective handling of a complaint when it is first reported is critical to avoiding EEOC complaints or litigation and will go a long way to ensure that employees feel that when they report inappropriate behavior to management, they are safe from retaliation and can expect some relief from the situation.

Conversely, the improper handling of a sexual harassment complaint, or worse, the failure to take the complaint seriously, can significantly impair the company's sexual harassment policy. Even worse, the resulting appearance of the policy's ineffectiveness can send the message that sexual harassing behavior is tolerated and carries no negative consequences for those who engage in such behaviors.

> *"The best defense is a good offense."*

Jack Dempsey, heavyweight prizefighter

Chapter 6
Investigating and resolving complaints: perhaps the key to an affirmative defense

Once the initial complaint has been made and handled properly, a neutral and objective individual, as designated by company policy, should conduct a detailed investigation.

Who Should Conduct the Investigation?
Needless to say, individuals involved in the complaint, their friends or close associates should never be involved in the investigation. This is generally easier in larger companies with an independent Human Resource or EEOC department staffed by individuals trained to conduct such investigations who may not even know the individuals involved in the complaint.

In smaller companies, it may be much more difficult to find an individual who can be completely neutral and objective. In either case, it would be appropriate to seek the assistance of an impartial third party outside the company who is experienced in conducting sexual harassment investigations. An independent investigator can function autonomously and is not subject to preconceived ideas and biases about individuals or the inner workings of the organization. As such, they are likely to be seen by all parties involved (including the courts) as impartial and unbiased information gatherers.

Regardless of who conducts the investigation, that individual should be well versed in what constitutes sexual harassment and the employer's responsibilities in such cases.

While the investigation is the employer's legal obligation, the investigator must consider the accuser's right to freedom from discrimination and harassment as well as the accused harasser's right to a full and fair investigation.

When Should the Investigation Begin?
In general, the investigation should begin as soon as possible. Unnecessarily delaying or extending the length of the investigation can have devastating effects on the organization and can also reduce witness reliability significantly.

The sooner the issue is resolved, the less time there is for gossip and speculation within the organization that may undermine productivity as well as potentially distort the perceptions of the situation in witnesses. Perhaps more importantly, the quicker the response, the lower the risk of litigation. Most employees don't file complaints so they can sue the company. They sue because the complaint was not handled properly, or even worse, not handled at all.

What If There is More Than One Allegation?
If more than one allegation exists against an individual or group, each allegation should be taken seriously and investigated *individually*. While the tendency might be to view separate events as being part of the same complaint, to do so would increase the possibility that a legitimate complaint would be ignored because the accompanying complaints do not constitute sexual harassment. The occurrence of a single sexually harassing event may tend to color the employee's view of subsequent events, leading them to see these as harassing as well.

Conversely, consideration of numerous events that would not, by themselves, be considered as harassing may influence our perception of the reliability of a legitimate complaint. Even though a complaint may appear frivolous on the surface, it should be treated as any other complaint and be investigated thoroughly. Keep in mind also that a number of minor incidents that, which taken individually might not be sufficient justification for a complaint, when taken together may establish a pattern sufficient to qualify as a hostile environment.

Confidentiality is Paramount

As with proper handling of the initial report, confidentiality is of paramount importance throughout the investigation. Information obtained in the process of the investigation should be released on a need-to-know basis only. It should be emphasized to all individuals involved in the investigation that discussions of the events surrounding the complaint should be kept confidential and limited to the context of the investigation.

Behavior contrary to these instructions should be considered as grounds for possible disciplinary action and all parties should be made aware of that. It is important to restrict release of this information in order to minimize the potentially disruptive influence this type of situation can have on the organization in general and on the individuals involved specifically. Premature release of information can also influence witness perceptions of the situation and, consequently, bias the findings of the investigation.

Review Personnel Files of the Parties Involved

Prior to interviewing any of the parties involved, the investigator should review the personnel files of the accuser and the accused harasser as well as any other files pertinent to this case. In addition, the investigator should prepare a preliminary list of questions based on the facts stated in the initial complaint. These questions should be directed at determining whether the reported sexual conduct actually occurred, whether it was unwelcome, and whether there is evidence of quid pro quo or hostile environment sexual harassment.

Steps Involved in Conducting Interviews

Inform all parties involved. When conducting interviews, the investigator should reiterate to the accuser, the accused, their supervisor(s), and any witnesses that the information gathered would be kept strictly confidential. The accuser and witnesses should be informed that no negative employment action will be taken against them as a result of making the complaint or participating in the investigation. The accuser and all witnesses should be instructed to report immediately any acts of retaliation or attempts at intimidation prior to or subsequent to their participation in the investigation.

All parties should be informed which individuals will have a legitimate need to know about the specific details of the investigation. They should be informed of the serious nature of the complaint and informed that the company will conduct a detailed investigation before reaching any conclusions or taking any remedial action. Additionally, all parties should be advised of the risk of defamation liability associated with making malicious or false allegations.

Encourage a detailed, written account. If possible, the employee filing the complaint should be encouraged to provide a detailed, written, signed account of the events that constitute the basis of the complaint. The investigator should make every effort to elicit specific details of these events with regard to the conduct, frequency, location, time frame, and specific context in which the behavior occurred.

Witnesses and other individuals who have reportedly experienced similar conduct by the accused should be identified and interviewed. These individuals should also be encouraged to provide a written account of any information they add to the investigation. Any additional documentation that might support this claim such as notes, letters, memos, email, pictures, etc., should be identified and obtained. With all of this information, a detailed chronology of events should be constructed to facilitate interpretation of the facts involved.

Determine the effects of the harassment. The investigator should attempt to determine the perceived effect of the harassing behavior on the individual filing the complaint. Specific effects such as fear, nightmares, sleep disruption, impairment of job performance, or reduced work opportunities should also be identified and substantiated when possible. If significant time elapsed between the occurrence and the actual report of the harassment, the investigator should endeavor to determine the reason for the delay in reporting the events. This line of inquiry may involve determining whether there were specific events that triggered the filing of the complaint and whether there were any possible motives on the part of the complainant for filing the complaint other than as a means of attaining relief from the situation.

Determine how the complainant would prefer the issue be resolved. The investigator should find out how that accuser would like to have the complaint resolved. Would the individual:

- Be satisfied if the accused were disciplined?
- Need to be moved to another job within the company?
- Be able to continue to work with that individual?
- Feel the need for counseling to reduce the effects of this situation on his or her life as well as job performance?

While it would be unwise to make promises about the outcome of the situation, it is still important to know what the individual expects as resolution of that situation.

Provide the accused enough information to respond to the complaint. When interviewing the accused harasser, that individual should be given enough information about the allegation(s) so that he or she can respond to the complaint. The individual should also be assured that a detailed investigation will be conducted before any remedial action is taken and that the details of the complaint will remain confidential in order to protect the rights of all parties concerned.

Determine the nature of the relationship between accuser and accused. The investigator should identify the nature of the existing relationship between the accuser and the accused. This should include the individual's position in the company, his or her level of responsibility and authority over the accuser, and the degree to which the individual can influence employment decisions affecting other employees including the accuser. Additionally, the nature of the social relationship between these individuals is of interest, particularly any prior consensual relationship including a history of individual or group socializing outside of the work environment.

Determine if the accused understands sexual harassment. In most cases, it would be reasonable to expect the accused harasser to deny the charges initially. This may be the result of ignorance of what constitutes sexual harassment or simply an attempt to avoid disciplinary action. The third possible alternative is that the allegations are false. It will be the task of the investigator to attempt to determine which explanation applies.

Ignorance of the law and what constitutes sexual harassment will likely be fairly easy to identify and rectify, whereas willful distortion of the facts on the part of any of the individuals involved constitutes a much more difficult problem to solve. In the absence of a simple explanation, the investigator should make every effort to explore with the accused the background, reasons and motivations for the allegations. Identify all documentation or witnesses to support the accused harasser's response to the allegations. As always, an effort should be made to obtain a written, signed account of this individual's response to the allegations if possible.

Interview supervisors of the parties involved. The respective supervisors of the parties involved should be interviewed to evaluate any prior discipline or behavioral problems that may be relevant to the allegations in this case. Of more importance, the investigator should try to determine if the supervisor(s) had any prior knowledge of the relationship between the parties or was aware of the reported harassing conduct. If the supervisor(s) knew of the reported inappropriate conduct or suspected the problem for any reason and failed to take the necessary action to remedy the situation, the company would be in an unsound position in litigation. Any documentation available that would support the investigator's findings in this area should be identified and obtained.

Ask open-ended questions. In the process of identifying witnesses to the alleged misconduct, release of the details of the allegations should be limited to open-ended questions designed to elicit that individual's account of what they saw or heard. The wording of questions can clearly influence the type of response the question evokes and can also reveal potentially damaging information about the individuals involved.

The question "Does John touch Mary inappropriately at the office?" tends to leave to interpretation what is meant by "inappropriate" and reveals too much detail about the allegation. In any case, wording of the question tends to bias the response to it. On the other hand, the question "Have you seen anyone touch Mary in a way that might make her uncomfortable?" will tend to elicit a more objective account of what that individual has observed or perhaps heard. This will also help the investigator determine whether the witnesses are providing information based on their own observations, gossip or hearsay. Once again, signed, written statements should be obtained if possible.

Evaluate the gathered facts. Once all of the interviews have been conducted and the available evidence has been collected, the investigator should attempt to evaluate the facts of the case. Did the alleged sexual conduct actually occur? If so, was it unwelcome? If the alleged sexual conduct actually occurred and it was unwelcome, does it constitute quid pro quo or hostile environment sexual harassment? And finally, did management make a reasonable effort to prevent the conduct or mediate the situation once they became aware of it? While the question of quid pro quo or hostile environment sexual harassment depends mainly upon fairly clear legal definitions, the other questions are much more subjective in nature.

Documented evidence is essential
Frequently, sexually harassing behavior occurs in private with few, if any, witnesses and little hard proof of its existence. All too often, it comes down to a matter of "he said" versus "she said" with little tangible evidence to support either side of the argument. This makes resolution of the situation difficult at best and leaves the company vulnerable to some form of litigation regardless of how it resolves the issue.

The bottom line is clear. Any determination resulting in any corrective action should be well founded and clearly supported by the facts gathered in the course of the investigation. "Gut instinct" is much more difficult to defend than a well-documented, carefully investigated conclusion supported by witness accounts, hard facts and tangible evidence

If the findings of the investigation clearly support the allegations, the company has a legal obligation to take immediate remedial action with respect to the harasser. Naturally, the severity of the harassment, the frequency with which it occurred, and the pervasiveness of the behavior should all be considered when determining the disciplinary action to be taken. The disciplinary action should eliminate the sexual harassment, and it should be taken immediately.

While there are a variety of disciplinary options available, ranging from oral or written warnings to discharge, any disciplinary action short of discharge should be accompanied by a written warning that similar misconduct in the future may be considered as grounds for immediate termination. In other words, if management decides to give the perpetrator a "second chance" for whatever reason, continued engagement in similar behaviors should be grounds for dismissal.

In addition, some form of remedial sexual harassment training might be appropriate and should include a review of the law and company policy. There are, obviously, a number of reasons that an organization might choose to keep someone accused of sexual harassment. Frequently, there is insufficient evidence supporting a complaint to justify termination. In other cases, the harassment is relatively minor in nature.

Probably the least valid reason for keeping someone who engages in sexually harassing behavior is the contribution they make to the bottom line. Admittedly, it is much easier to terminate someone who is easily replaced than it is to terminate the company's most productive salesperson. Nonetheless, the last thing the company needs is to continue to employ an individual with a history of engaging in sexually harassing behavior. Not only does that leave the company open to liability in litigation for failing to make a reasonable effort to eliminate sexual harassment, but it also undermines the credibility of the company's sexual harassment policy.

If the findings of the investigation show the allegations to be false, every effort should be made to determine whether the individual simply misinterpreted the conduct as sexually harassing or willfully lied in making the allegations. If it is determined that the accuser lied, the investigator should have clear support for this prior to taking any disciplinary action for filing a false report. The disciplining of an individual who mistakenly reported sexual harassment can discourage other employees from reporting instances of sexual harassment as well as leave the company liable for retaliating against someone who reports sexual harassment.

In any case, discipline should not be imposed unless there is clear evidence that the individual was fully aware that they were filing a false claim. It is also recommended that the company carefully review this option with legal counsel prior to taking any disciplinary action. Having met that criterion, discipline should be consistent with company policy concerning dishonesty.

Regardless, of whether the investigation finds the allegations to be true or false, the determination of whether or not the respective supervisors involved in the case were aware of the situation is important for several reasons. First of all, the mere fact that the investigation looked at the effectiveness of the company's mechanisms to prevent sexual harassment would support the company's claim that a reasonable effort had been made to eliminate and/or remediate sexual harassment. Secondly, this gives the company an opportunity to evaluate the effectiveness of its sexual harassment policy training within management and possibly identify areas that need attention.

Finally, this gives upper management an opportunity to assess the degree to which lower levels of management "buy into" the company's sexual harassment policy. Needless to say, a supervisor or manager that does not act in accordance with the company's sexual harassment policy leaves the company vulnerable to litigation.

Most importantly, DOCUMENT, DOCUMENT, and DOCUMENT! Document everything that is said and done in the course of the investigation. If possible, written transcripts should be made of all interviews conducted. This "paper trail" may be the only support for the company's claim that they made "a reasonable effort" to prevent or correct sexual harassment.

"Follow the habit of asking 'How do you know?' Never accept opinion as fact. Don't trust information given in a discourteous or slanderous spirit. In asking for information, do not disclose what you wish the information to be."

Unknown

Chapter 7
Some final thoughts

In spite of the potential consequences and the almost obsessive media coverage of high profile cases over the last ten years, sexual harassment is still "alive and well" in many organizations. It is, obviously, not for lack of effort on the part of most companies. While there are still companies that never seem to get around to updating their sexual harassment policy or scheduling sexual harassment awareness training for their employees, most organizations are making a legitimate attempt to prevent harassment. Unfortunately, as long as people find themselves working in close proximity to one another, the potential for sexual harassment exists. That statement seems as true today as it did when this book was originally written in 2000.

This book lays out some of the fundamental things organizations can do to protect themselves against potential liability in litigation. Basically, having an effective sexual harassment policy, clearly communicating that policy to all employees, handling and resolving complaints fairly and promptly will likely meet the minimum requirements for establishing an affirmative defense in the case of litigation.

Still, this is only the beginning of the process. The best way to protect against litigation liability is to provide employees with a sexual harassment-free workplace. This requires a commitment from every level of management to enforce policy and display a zero tolerance stance against those types of behaviors. Additionally, management must be committed to an ongoing training process that creates an awareness of sexual harassing behaviors and fosters mutual respect among employees.

If your organization has fifteen or more employees, it is subject to federal law and in many states, as few as four employees makes the organization responsible under state law for preventing sexual harassment and other forms of discrimination.

Appendix A
Supreme Court Rulings

While there have been a number of significant court cases concerning sexual harassment in the years since Title VII of the Civil Rights Act of 1964 came into existence, the U.S. Supreme Court has only addressed the issue eight times. The last of those cases was decided in 2006. What follows is a very brief summary of each of those cases, the decisions handed down by the Court, and the implications of those decisions.

MERITOR SAVINGS BANK v. VINSON, 477 U.S. 57 (1986)
Mechelle Vinson worked at the same branch of the Meritor Savings Bank for four years, advancing from teller-trainee to teller to head teller to assistant branch manager. In September of 1978 she notified her supervisor, Sidney Taylor, that she was taking sick leave for an indefinite period. On November 1, 1978, the bank discharged her for excessive use of that leave. She then brought action against Taylor and the bank claiming that she had "constantly been subjected to sexual harassment" by Taylor in violation of Title VII.

Ms. Vinson indicated that after her probationary period as a teller-trainee, Taylor invited her to dinner and subsequently suggested they go to a motel to have sexual relations. She stated that she eventually agreed out of fear of losing her job. She further alleged that Taylor made continued demands upon her for sexual favors and estimated that she had sexual intercourse with him 40 to 50 times over the next several years.

The Court ruled that a woman who submitted to the sexual advances of her boss any number of times because she feared losing her job could sue for sexual harassment. The Court also ruled that an employer could be held liable for sexual harassment committed by supervisors if it knew or should have known about the conduct and did nothing to correct it. The implication of this ruling is that it doesn't matter if the employee submitted voluntarily but whether the supervisor's advances were unwelcome. This ruling makes employers liable in virtually all cases of *quid pro quo* sexual harassment.

HARRIS v. FORKLIFT SYSTEMS, INC., 92-1168 (1993)

Teresa Harris worked as a manager at Forklift Systems, Inc., for approximately two and a half years. Charles Hardy was the company president during that time. Ms. Harris claimed that Hardy often made gender-related insults and made her the frequent target of unwanted sexual innuendos. She indicated that she complained to him about his conduct and he said he was only joking and apologized. The behavior reportedly stopped for a while but then resumed. Shortly thereafter, Harris quit and sued Forklift Systems claiming that Hardy had created a hostile work environment for her because of her gender.

The Court ruled that even if a discriminatorily abusive work environment does not affect the individual's psychological well being, it is unlawful and a violation of Title VII. The implication of this ruling is that it is enough that the employee perceives the work environment as hostile and the abusive conduct is severe or pervasive enough that a reasonable person would find it to be hostile.

LANDGRAF v. USI FILM PRODUCTS, 511 U.S. 244 (1994)

Barbara Landgraf was employed by USI Film Products for approximately fifteen months. She reported that a fellow employee named John Williams repeatedly harassed her through inappropriate remarks and physical contact. Her complaints to her immediate supervisor were ignored. When she complained to the personnel manager, action was taken and Williams was transferred to another department. Landgraf quit her job four days later and subsequently sued USI Film Products.

A District Court found that Williams had sexually harassed her but that since the company had remedied the situation and she was not unlawfully discharged, she was not entitled to equitable relief. Since Title VII did not authorize any other form of relief at that time, her case was dismissed.

While her case was awaiting appeal, the Civil Rights Act of 1991 was signed into law. As this Act creates a right to recover compensatory and punitive damages for certain violations of Title VII, the Supreme Court reviewed the case to determine if those provisions applied to a case pending on appeal when the law was passed. The Court ruled that the findings of the lower courts were consistent with the provisions of the law in effect at the time. Therefore, the enactment of the new law was not retroactive to cases filed and decided prior to that enactment.

ONCALE v. SUNDOWNER OFFSHORE SERVICES, INC., No. 96-568 (1998)

Joseph Oncale was employed by Sundowner Offshore Services as a roustabout on an oil platform in the Gulf of Mexico. He claimed that on several occasions, he was forcibly subjected to sex-related, humiliating actions by his supervisor and two fellow employees. He also alleged physical assault in a sexual manner and threats of rape. His complaints to supervisory personnel were ignored and Mr. Oncale eventually quit. He filed a complaint against Sundowner alleging that he was discriminated against because of his sexual orientation in violation of Title VII.

The Court ruled that men as well as women can file sexual harassment claims under Title VII. The Court also ruled that same sex harassment is unlawful under Title VII. The implication of this ruling is that men are equally protected under the provisions of Title VII regardless of their sexual orientation.

FARAGHER v. CITY OF BOCA RATON, No. 97-282 (1998)

For approximately five years Beth Ann Faragher worked part time and during the summers as an ocean lifeguard for the City of Boca Raton, Florida. During that time, her immediate supervisors were Bill Terry and David Silverman. She resigned in 1990 and subsequently brought an action against Terry, Silverman and the City alleging that Terry and Silverman created a sexually hostile work environment by repeatedly subjecting her and other female lifeguards to lewd and offensive remarks and gestures and by unwelcome physical contact. Ms. Faragher never reported this contact to any city official. Although the City had a sexual harassment policy in place, it had failed to disseminate it to all employees, most notably the lifeguards.

While the actions of the two supervisors were clearly unlawful under Title VII, the question of the circumstances under which an employer is liable for the acts of a supervisor who creates a hostile work environment is at issue. The Court ruled that an employer is responsible for the acts of a supervisor that results in a hostile environment but considers an affirmative defense based on the reasonableness of the employer's conduct as well as that of the complaining employee.

The implication of this ruling is that an employer may be able to avoid liability in hostile environment cases involving a manager where no tangible employment action occurs.

BURLINGTON INDUSTRIES v. ELLERTH, No. 97-569 (1998)
For fifteen months Kimberly Ellerth worked as a salesperson in one of the many divisions of Burlington Industries. One of her supervisors, Ted Slowik, was a mid-level manager who had the authority to hire and promote employees subject to higher authority. Ms. Ellerth alleged that Slowik repeatedly subjected her to boorish and offensive remarks and gestures. She cited three specific incidents where his remarks could be considered threats to deny her tangible job benefits. She refused all of his advances but never suffered tangible retaliation and was promoted once.

She never reported the harassment despite knowing that Burlington had a policy against sexual harassment. She eventually quit her job and filed suit against Burlington claiming sexual harassment that forced her constructive discharge.

The Court reviewed the case to decide whether an employee who refuses the unwelcome advances of a supervisor, and yet suffers no tangible job consequences, can recover damages against an employer for the supervisor's actions without proving negligence or other fault.

---

*Vicariously Liable: When one person is liable for the negligent actions of another person, even though the first person was not directly responsible for the injury.

The Court ruled that the employer was *vicariously liable** if a supervisor creates a sexually hostile workplace regardless of evidence of adverse, tangible employment consequences. The implication of this ruling is that employers are generally held liable if a supervisor is involved regardless of the type of sexual harassment that occurs. The company may still have an affirmative defense, meaning they can prove they did everything possible to prevent or remedy the situation.

What Does It Mean?

In these last two cases, the Court minimized the difference between quid pro quo and hostile environment. It also established a new rule for determining employer liability. Under this new rule, the employer is liable if a supervisor creates a hostile environment and if adverse, tangible employment action results. In the absence of such employment action, the employer is still liable unless:

- the employer has taken what the Court describes as reasonable care to prevent sexual harassment and to promptly remedy any incidents that occur, and
- the employee unreasonably refused to use an established procedure to report the occurrence of such incidents.

The conclusion that should be drawn from these rulings is that employers have to take all steps necessary to prevent and remedy promptly any incidents of sexual harassment. Even if they do that, they can still be held liable for incidents of hostile environment harassment involving a manager if the victim files a complaint

BURLINGTON NORTHERN & SANTA FE RAILWAY CO. v WHITE, No. 05-259 (2006)

Sheila White was interviewed in June of 1997 by Marvin Brown, the roadmaster for the Burlington Northern & Santa Fe Railroad Company. Brown expressed interest in her previous experience operating forklifts and hired her as a "track laborer" in the Maintenance of Way Department at Burlington's Tennessee yard. She was the only woman working at that location. The track laborer position involves maintenance, repair and upkeep of the right-of-way.

Soon after Ms. White started at the Tennessee yard, the individual who had previously operated the forklift took another position and Brown immediately assigned her to operate the forklift. While she also performed other duties associated with the track laborer position, her primary duty was operating the forklift.

In September of 1997, Ms. White complained to Burlington's management that her immediate supervisor had made insulting and inappropriate remarks to her in front of her male co-workers. She also complained that he repeatedly told her that women should not be working in that department. Burlington investigated and suspended the supervisor for ten days and made him attend a sexual harassment training session.

When Brown informed Ms. White of the supervisor's discipline he also informed her that she was being removed from forklift duty and would only perform standard track laborer tasks. Brown said the reassignment was in response to complaints from her co-workers that "a more senior man" should have the "less arduous and cleaner job."

In October of that year Ms. White filed a complaint with the EEOC claiming that her reassignment was gender-based discrimination and retaliation for her earlier complaint. In December she filed an additional complaint with the EEOC stating that Brown had "placed her under surveillance" and was monitoring her daily activities.

Shortly after filing the second complaint Ms. White had a disagreement with her new supervisor who reported to Brown that she had been insubordinate. Brown immediately suspended her without pay. Ms. White then filed an internal grievance which resulted in her being reinstated and receiving back pay for the 37 days she was suspended. She filed an additional retaliation charge with the EEOC based on the suspension.

Ms. White filed suit in federal court claiming that Burlington had unlawfully retaliated against her by changing her job responsibilities and by suspending her for 37 days. The jury awarded her $43,500 in compensatory damages which was affirmed on appeal.

The U.S. Supreme Court heard this case to clarify the standard for whether the retaliation has to be employment or workplace related and just how harmful it must be. The Court ruled that retaliation did not have to be confined to tangible employment actions but did require a retaliation plaintiff to show that the challenged action *'well might have dissuaded a reasonable worker from making or supporting a charge of discrimination.'* The Court also found that a reassignment of job duties could constitute retaliation even though the new duties fell within the existing job description.

The implication of this ruling is that almost any action taken against an individual who files a harassment complaint can be considered retaliation if that action would dissuade a reasonable employee from filing a complaint.

PENNSYLVANIA STATE POLICE v SUDERS, 542 U. S. 129 (2004)

Nancy Suders was hired as a police communications operator for a unit of the Pennsylvania State Police. She was subjected to what the Court described as "a continuous barrage of sexual harassment that ceased only when she left the force" by three male supervisors. The behaviors included graphic sex talk, obscene gestures and actions, verbal abuse and physical intimidation.

Three months after she was hired she was accused of taking an accident file home with her. She approached the Equal Employment Opportunity office and said she may need some help. Eight weeks later she informed the EEO officer that she was being harassed and that she was afraid. The EEO officer told her to file a complaint but did not provide the appropriate form and did not tell her how to get the form.

Shortly after that, she was arrested for stealing test papers from her computer proficiency test. She had been repeatedly told that she had failed the computer proficiency test each time she took it though she had begun to suspect that the exams were not even being graded. She had located the papers and taken them out to be reviewed.

She was arrested when she tried to return the papers. She was handcuffed, given her Miranda rights and interrogated. At that point she asked that she be able to resign and provided a written resignation she had prepared previously. She was eventually released and no theft charges were ever filed against her.

She subsequently filed suit with the District Court alleging sexual harassment in violation of Title VII and also claimed constructive discharge. The Court ruled that the State Police was not vicariously liable because Ms. Suders had not availed herself of the procedures in place for reporting sexual harassment. On appeal the Circuit Court reversed the ruling and held that constructive discharge was a tangible employment action and therefore the affirmative defense was not available.

The U.S. Supreme Court heard the case to resolve the issue of whether constructive discharge would preclude the availability of the affirmative defense to the employer in a hostile environment case involving a supervisor. The Court ruled that in the absence of any official act on the part of the employer, the affirmative defense would be available.

The implication of this ruling is that employers are strictly liable for the acts of a supervisor if a tangible employment action results in a constructive discharge. In the absence of a tangible employment action, the employer may be able to avoid liability through the affirmative defense

Appendix B
Sample Sexual Harassment Policy

The following sample policy is provided as a simple template for use in developing an effective sexual harassment policy. It contains the basic essential elements described in the previous chapters. Since each business has its own specific characteristics, this policy should be adapted to reflect the nature of the organization. This may entail removing items in some cases and adding new items in others. **Under no circumstances, should this be construed as a substitute for competent legal counsel.**

HARASSMENT POLICY

It is the policy of the Company to maintain a working environment which encourages mutual respect, promotes respectful and congenial relationships between employees and is free from all forms of illegal harassment of any employee or applicant for employment by anyone, including managers, co-workers, vendors, customers, or independent contractors. Illegal harassment in any manner or form is expressly prohibited and will not be tolerated by the Company. Accordingly, Company management is committed to vigorously enforcing this policy against harassment -- including but not limited to sexual harassment -- at all levels within the Company.

All reported or suspected occurrences of illegal harassment will be promptly and thoroughly investigated. Where illegal harassment is determined to have occurred, the Company will immediately take appropriate disciplinary action, including written warnings, suspension, transfer and/or termination. Employees also may have personal liability for behavior that violates state and federal anti-harassment laws.

The Company will not permit or condone any acts of retaliation against anyone who files harassment complaints or cooperates in the investigation of reported or suspected occurrences of harassment.

Also, it is unlawful for employers to retaliate against employees who oppose the practices prohibited by the Equal Employment Opportunity Commission (EEOC), or file complaints, or otherwise participate in an investigation, proceeding, or hearing conducted by the EEOC. Similarly, the Company prohibits employees from hindering its own internal investigations and its internal complaint procedure.

The term "harassment" includes but is not limited to unwelcome slurs, jokes, verbal, graphic or physical conduct relating to an individual's race, color, religious creed, sex, national origin, ancestry, citizenship status, pregnancy, physical disability, mental disability, age, military status or status as a Vietnam-era or special disabled veteran, marital status, registered domestic partner status, gender (including sex stereotyping), medical condition (including, but not limited to, cancer related or HIV/AIDS related) or sexual orientation.

Sexual harassment consists of unwelcome sexual advances, requests for sexual favors, or other verbal or physical conduct of a sexual nature where:

- Submission to such conduct is an explicit or implicit term or condition of employment;
- Employment decisions are based on an employee's submission to or rejection of such conduct; or
- Such conduct interferes with an individual's work performance or creates an intimidating, hostile or offensive working environment.

Sexual harassment is specifically prohibited regardless of whether it rises to the level of a legal violation. Examples of sexual and/or gender-based harassment prohibited by this policy include:

- Offensive sex-oriented verbal kidding, teasing or jokes;
- Repeated unwanted sexual flirtations, advances or propositions;
- Verbal abuse of a sexual nature;

- Graphic or degrading comments about an individual's appearance or sexual activity;

- Offensive visual conduct, including leering, making sexual gestures, the display of offensive sexually suggestive objects or pictures, cartoons or posters;

- Unwelcome pressure for sexual activity;

- Offensively suggestive or obscene letters, notes or invitations; or

- Offensive physical contact such as patting, grabbing, pinching, or brushing against another's body. Violations of this policy will result in disciplinary action up to and including termination.

The term "harassment" may also include conduct of employees, supervisors, vendors and/or customers who engage in verbally or physically harassing behavior that has the potential for humiliating or embarrassing an employee of the Company based on the protected categories listed above.

Complaint Procedure

The Company provides its employees with a convenient and reliable method for reporting incidents of harassment, including sexual harassment. Any employee who feels that they have been or are being harassed or discriminated against, is encouraged to immediately inform the alleged harasser that the behavior is unwelcome. In most instances, the person is unaware that their conduct is offensive and when so advised can easily and willingly correct the conduct so that it does not reoccur.

If the informal discussion with the alleged harasser is unsuccessful in remedying the problem, or if such an approach is either not possible or comfortable for the employee, the employee should immediately report the complained-of conduct to his or her immediate supervisor, on-site manager, or if necessary for resolution, to Human Resources. If for any reason the employee does not feel comfortable reporting the complaint to anyone else, he or she may go directly to the Human Resource Department. The report should include all facts available to the employee regarding the harassment.

Confidentiality

All reports of harassment will be treated seriously. However, absolute confidentiality is not promised nor can it be assured. The Company will conduct an investigation of any complaint and that will require limited disclosure of pertinent information to certain parties, including the alleged harasser.

Investigative Procedure

Once a complaint is received, the Company will begin a prompt and thorough investigation. The investigation may include interviews with all involved employees, including the alleged harasser, and any employees who are aware of facts or incidents alleged to have occurred. The Company prohibits employees from hindering an internal investigation or the internal complaint procedure.

Once the investigation is completed, a determination will be made regarding the appropriate response to the allegations. If it is determined that a violation of the harassment policy has occurred, prompt, remedial action will be taken. This may include some or all of the following steps:

- Restore any lost terms, conditions or benefits of employment to the complaining employee.
- Discipline the harasser. This discipline can include written disciplinary warnings, transfer, demotion, suspension, and termination.
- If the harassment is from a vendor or customer, the Company will take appropriate action to stop the complained-of conduct.

The EEOC may also investigate and process complaints of harassment. Violators are subject to penalties and remedial measures that may include sanctions, fines, injunctions, reinstatement, back pay, and damages. The address of the local EEOC office can be found among the state and federal office listings in the telephone book.

Duties of Employees and Managers

All employees of the Company, both management and non-management, are responsible for assuring that a workplace free of illegal harassment is maintained. Any employee may file a harassment complaint regarding incidents experienced personally or incidents observed in the workplace. The Company strives to maintain a lawful, pleasant work environment where all employees are able to effectively perform their work without interference of any type and requests the assistance of all employees in this effort.

All Company supervisors and managers are expected to adhere to the Company's anti-harassment policy. All managers and supervisors are responsible for doing all they can to prevent and discourage illegal harassment from occurring. If a complaint is raised, supervisors and managers are to act promptly and to notify the Human Resources of the complaint so that it may proceed with an investigation. If a supervisor or manager fails to follow this policy, they will receive appropriate disciplinary action up to and including termination.

References

American Bar Association. 1997. *ABA Guide to Workplace Law: Everything you need to know about your rights as an employee or employer.* Times Books. New York, NY.

Andrew, M.J. & Andrew, J.D. 1997. Sexual harassment Part 3: Internal policies, practices, and procedures. *Journal of Rehabilitation Administration.* 21 (3), 151-167.

Blumenthal, J.A. 1998. The reasonable woman standard: A meta-analytic review of gender differences in perceptions of sexual harassment. *Law and Human Behavior,* 22, 33-57.

Deadrick, D.L, Kezman, S.W. & McAfee, R.B. Harassment by nonemployers: How should employers respond? *HR Magazine.* December, 1996.

Deschenaux, Joanne. EEOC: Train Managers on Harassment. *HR Magazine.* May 2008.

Fitzgerald, L.F. 1993. Sexual Harassment: Violence against women in the workplace. *American Psychologist,* 48, 1070-1076.

Fitzgerald, L.F., Drasgow, F., Hulin, C.L., Gelfand, M.J., & Magley, V.J. 1997. Antecedents and consequences of sexual harassment in organizations: A test of an integrated model. *Journal of Applied Psychology,* 82, 578-589.

Gardener, B.A, 2004. *Black's Law Dictionary, 8th Ed.* Thompson West.

Gibson, P.C. & Johnson, M.A. 1998. *Sexual Harassment Prevention Training Manual For Managers and Supervisors.* CCH, Inc. Chicago.

Gruber, J.E. 1998. The impact of male work environments and organizational policies on women's experiences of sexual harassment. *Gender & Society.* 12, 301-320.

Jarin, K.M. New rules for same sex harassment. *HR Magazine.* June 1998.

Klein, Karen E. Training Can Keep Companies Out of Court. *Business Week Online.* 3/9/2006, P1-1.

Moore, H.I., Gatlin-Watts, R.W. & Cangelosi, J. 1998. Eight steps to a sexual harassment-free workplace. *Training & Development.* April 1998.

Murray, B. 1998. Psychology's voice in sexual harassment law. *APA Monitor.* 29, 8.

Segal, J.A. Prevent now or pay later. *HR Magazine.* October 1998.

Segal, J.A. The catch-22s of remedying sexual harassment complaints. *HR Magazine.* October 1997.

Supreme Court of the United States. *MERITOR SAVINGS BANK v. VINSON, 477 U.S. 57 (1986).*

Supreme Court of the United States. *HARRIS v. FORKLIFT SYSTEMS, INC., 92-1168 (1993).*

Supreme Court of the United States. *LANDGRAF v. USI FILM PRODUCTS, 511 U.S. 244 (1994).*

Supreme Court of the United States. *ONCALE v. SUNDOWNER OFFSHORE SERVICES, INC., No. 96-568 (1998).*

Supreme Court of the United States. *FARAGHER v. CITY OF BOCA RATON, No. 97-282 (1998).*

Supreme Court of the United States. *BURLINGTON INDUSTRIES v. ELLERTH, No. 97-569 (1998).*

Supreme Court of the United States. *BURLINGTON NORTHERN & SANTA FE RAILWAY CO. v WHITE, No. 05-259 (2006).*

Supreme Court of the United States. *PENNSYLVANIA STATE POLICE v SUDERS, 542 U. S. 129 (2004).*

U.S. Equal Employment Opportunity Commission (EEOC). 1990. Policy Guidance on Current Issues of Sexual Harassment. (Notice M-915-050) Washington, D.C.: Government Printing Office.

U.S. Equal Employment Opportunity Commission (EEOC). 2008. Harassment Charges FY 1997 - FY 2007. http://www.eeoc.gov/stats/harassment.html.